FARE WELL
~
BEIR BEANNACHT

Poems in English and Irish

RITA KELLY

ATTIC PRESS

First published by
Attic Press
44 East Essex Street
Dublin 2

British Library Cataloguing in Publication Data
Kelly, Rita
  Fare well (Beir beannacht).
  I. Title
  821.914

  ISBN 0-946211-66-3

Cover Design: Paula Nolan
Typesetting: Phototype-Set Ltd., Dublin
Printing: Billings

This book is published with the assistance of the Arts Council/An Comhairle Ealaíon, Ireland.

But there come times — perhaps this is one of them —
when we have to take ourselves more seriously or die;
when we have to pull back from the incantations,
rhythms we've moved to thoughtlessly,
and disenthrall ourselves . . .

Adrienne Rich *Transcendental Etude*

FOR NORA
whose friendship is as
steadfast as Chimborazo

ACKNOWLEDGEMENTS

The author and publishers would like to thank the Arts Council/An Chomhairle Ealaíon and Bord na Gaeilge for their assistance.

Acknowledgements are due to the following magazines and newspapers in which some of these poems have appeared: *The Irish Press; Hibernia; Riverine; Departures; Innti; Poetry Ireland Review; Comhar; Feasta; Grapevine; Women's Studies International Forum; Tijdschrift voor Poezie.* And also to: Ciarán Ó Coigligh, Editor, *An Fhiliocht Chomhaimsearta 1975-1985,* Coiscéim, 1987; Ailbhe Smyth, Editor, *Wildish Things: An Anthology of New Irish Women's Writing,* Attic Press, 1989; Adrian Moynes, Producer, *The Poet's Eye,* RTE, 1989; Pádraig Ó Snodaigh, Director, Coiscéim: *Dialann sa Díseart,* 1981 and *An Bealach Éadóigh,* 1984.

Contents

I

Naming the Scent of Roses

Today, a friend sent me
one of her stories
set in a marginalised community
in Ecuador,
where people with strange names
— Zoila, Manuela, Hernan —
are carried by sweating mules
up mountains, and 'slither towards
eternity on the downward path'.
Where an old woman knows
that her two sons will come
before her corpse has cooled
to pull down her house,
and fight about who should
have the door,
and who the beams.
And she knows too
that her sons' wives will claw each other
over her pot, her enamel plate,
and her single spoon.
Her clothes are worthless,
though homespun, once they defied the sun
in bright squares of red, green and turquoise.
But now the colours are faded
from her clothes
just as the smooth beauty of youth
has drained itself in channels from her face:
so her sons and their women
will take her old clothes
and burn them with the thatch —
These things which have protected her
from an infernal sun —
and her corpse will have grown cold.
The story tells of youth too,
it tells of hair which gleams
'black-blue' as the hairs on your head
do, at evening when we stand silent for a second

despite the rush-hour traffic
outside your gate,
despite the windows of suburbia
upon us like lidless eyes
you pluck a rose, quite painlessly,
and offer it,
that I might not go out
from the edge of this clearing
empty-handed and unknowing.
We draw near to catch the scent,
it pervades and permeates
until there is only it and you.
I have no name for this moment.
Your eyes look straight into mine
and I have no name for that either,
but my friend's story from Ecuador
tells me that they are 'sherry red',
or maybe it's sherry brown.

As I join the ebb and flow of traffic
I catch sight of you
in the rear-view mirror, eyes downcast,
and I wonder
do you fear that all we have packed
into short periods of exquisite pleasure
will slip and wither or,
do you fear that it is all already
slipping and withering
without a name?
What of the story from Ecuador?
It tells of love growing thin
and being ground down to a single spoon,
as I reach the story's end
I know, when I speak your name,
or when I hear your voice,
mellow in the naming of itself
that our story has not yet
found its end.

Kew Gardens

'*the voice cried aloud*
and the petals of myriads of flowers flashed their
colours into the air.'
— Virginia Woolf *Kew Gardens.*

There are no white butterflies now
rambling vaguely or dancing
one above another, but then
it is not July,
no, it is March, bright and clear
and rather cold.

Always the voices,
yet I do not hear yours
or your laugh as Bowen heard it
the February before
you filled your pockets
with stones and walked
into it, out of it.

No, it is a different voice
and embodied, right close by,
clear as a March morning
and full of enthusiasms.
We share fragments of a packed past
and have come from opposite ends
of the earth, so it seems,
and yet that bond,
that trust that neither
you nor I shall use
stones to sink ourselves
in these uneasy times.

R.S.V.P.

Your secret place is off the coast,
an island, with a causeway too it seems.
And there are drifts of wings
and flower-scent on the breeze —
a warm luxurious breeze.
You will go there and lie along your back,
absorbing the far depths of an immense sky.
Clouds will come, coloured shadows, coming slowly
and determinedly out of the unseen.
Surreptitiously the tide fills at your feet
and sleeks its way along your limbs
you are tense against its rise and hold down
until sea and sky and sun are one unspeakable experience
of release.

Your hair is stranded out,
your eyes fixed forever —
and all the pain is unleashed.

But no, I cannot lie there with you
some high summer's day
and feel the fill of the water at my feet
before dissolving in an immensity of sky.
I cannot halt the tide
or raise your island out of that vast inundation:
I can only hold you on this sharp spring day
and let you cry.

Granard

I have driven against the blue light of dawn,
and slept eventually in a strange room;
but my mind rushes back along the miles,
back to you.
There are some over-riding images
which haunt a little, there is some relief too,
as if I had to go out into this vacant
and unfriendly night
to wake and find a truth.

Perhaps this is my letter from the Black Sea,
feeling, like Ovid, frustrated,
banished from Rome, I write again,
and again hope that you might
give up the stubborn power of Augustus,
and that I might, in this century,
come within sight of you.

Forgive me too if this seems like an abstract,
the summary which shortens to the essential.
It is my attempt to speak your language,
having demanded for so long
that you should speak mine.

My arrogance is a wall
I have built and capped
with broken glass
to protect my empty backyard,
and the bits and pieces of possessions,
memories mostly and distances of mind
which reach back into all
that has formed me.

I identified myself for the night porter,
told him I was his late arrival.

Finding me, I feel, unthreatening,
he offers conversation by asking
if I had come from Dublin,
was it work that had delayed me?
Of course I could not say
that it was simply you,
and that dinner was delightful,
and that it had trailed into a long line
of brandies as we tried to recapture
in the candlelight all that we had lost,
and hold it before the dawn would take
it all away again brutally.

I could not tell this night porter
that we left the waiter our respective
payments and a line of empty glasses
and moved out into the city
with so much still unsaid.

Or that he had heard your voice hours ago
arrange with him the details of my arrival —
thoughtful always — though we sat
for hours after at the mouth of a cul-de-sac,
and watched cats prowl and pick their way
along the edge of houses.

It is morning now
and the rain is soaking this town.
The paint peels from the narrow frontages,
there is a narrowness about this place
which culminates in the church spire.
There are milk lorries and articulated trucks,
and a young woman pushes a pram across
the street, she wears red high-heeled shoes
and no stockings, I can feel the rain on
her bare legs.

Another woman, in wellingtons, carries
a quarter of beef into a butcher's stall,
it fills her outstretched arms and weighs
upon her; she has a mothering face,
she might well have mothered us
some spring morning with warm milk,
but now she holds a piece of dead meat
to her breast.

Like the small towns I belong to,
this place too is characterised by a hunger.
I feel strange here,
something tightens in my throat,
and there is you, and the fear
that we might wake to find our love
stillborn under a statue.

High-Altitude Species

We have pushed to where the pigeons
are undisturbed, and sent them shocked
feathering the branches of the upper world.
And we have foresaken the evening
and thrown the countryside into relief
creating the far-off mountains, towns too,
homesteads with their neat boundary lines
are enclosed beneath us.

A stand of fir trees infirms us,
rooting itself for the next century,
solidly shaping beams for the unborn
to span a time we can never reach.
Yet, we let it slip beyond us
and gladly give because we know
that we are late-comers to the world,
and the world holds us
but a moment in its slow
and deliberate movement.

September Solo

Home is harmony
movement in a composed place,
extemporising to all the termini
within the stays and struts of symphony.

That gathering twitter
I know, the swallowed sky:
it is but the melody of quittance
to find a ship worth charter.

The leaves too modulate,
a chromatic, chartaceous cadence,
flit and slip the intervals of habit
through an air no longer estivate.

Perhaps they'll strike a chord,
transition to the warm, and fly
to escape the year's void,
leaving the diminished nest exposed.

And because I stay
I am become the away.

The Archbishop is Dead

I turn from this city
hearing that he wished
to be remembered
in Christian love —
so we have remembered him
as you read those strong melodic lines
in a friendly time before noon.
There comes a time for each of us
to put on the 'absurd flippers,
the grave and awkward mask'
and crawl down into the depths,
and salvage ourselves from the wreck.

There is no anger left for the Archbishop
and all his decent dogma,
despite the pomp and the glory
it is all rendered powerless
in the harsh terms of this universe.
There is only the radio-voice
and the unintended sound-effects
of the palace clock chiming
through the interview:
perhaps that clock is a glass dome,
a belljar, with sparkling brass orbs
making the half-circle?
A kind of clock
fit for a cleric.

Poor man, he has died in state,
hopefully not in sin, and his voice tires
on the airwaves, always the moral question.
He might have been yet more happy
with his dearly loved books
than holding position.

There comes an ease
within your room,
and within the bodies
we find ourselves in
on such a day as this
with no position to hold.

Chiaroscuro

Snowdrops are rumours,
windows inanimate things,
as for foxgloves, one has heard how they loom
along pathways in Wicklow places,
bee-bodies, mottled against the sun.

There are deckchairs and fireplaces
rooftops and walls which hold in:
dykes against an inundation of sky.
One has had reports of waves
forming themselves in gray linear patterns
along the western coasts,
and glum stone walls extend that pattern —
on the old seafloor we take shelter
against the wind, and a gull stands watch.

Such things remain rumours of the real,
reports of the unrealised.

Until the composing eye catches and clarifies.
Through a slight stroke, a tint of definition
we recognise
the thing itself.

Goodbye

Why can't it be some well-defined,
explicit phrase: plain and unequivocal?
Something which cuts clean
leaving no jagged edges, no spillages?

Then perhaps the scent of roses and their opulence
would not mar a late summer evening
when the sun is burnishing the grass
before the world lets it slip.
And a bee's wing resounding
against the petal-walls is a terrifying thing.

Why must you push through the humus
of memory in Spring —
why can't the dormant bulbs lie, or die,
in the cold earth? Would we miss the
crocus and the humble snowdrop,
or is it only the association that we miss
the moment of shared apperception,
the tender connotation — yes, that
Spring, and that Spring and the Spring
of such and such a year, what we did,
and what we hoped to do
and how you wore your hair . . .
but nothing erases the image
from the retinae.

You are always there, even in the small monies
carefully collected, the little sacrifices
which are made automatically, only to be
scattered without aim, and your birth in Spring
goes unmarked.

Shop-windows are full of meaningless possibility —
there is no surmise, no interior debate
no offering of the saved pounds and the pence
in that moment of breathless choice,
and all birthday cards are an outrage.

Language plays its old tricks,
seems adequate, decisive:
but there is no semantic
to eradicate you from the heart.

A Hanseatic City

I would like to leave you the world
and go out into this flake-filled morning
and gather yet more worlds for you
from places touched and untouched
by this snow that has stolen down
upon us.
I would like to bind them lovingly in one volume.

Yes we know our Dante, we have taken
diverse paths to the Paradiso, though
the hell moments have held us too
in this sometimes dolorous city.

But I will remember you
and how the dull-creamed
light of snow drained the colour
from your face and eyes.
I will remember too
the things you could not say
of how you knew me
and all that had passed in between
being born and finding you
brilliant among books.

Woman's Plight upon the Planet

What do we care for the hoar moon
pulling at our potentials
to solve for the time being
our inner delicacies?

Night, our matrix,
we of the darker prospects
are motherbound
and our genius is cold light.

Spent in the expansiveness
ebb, flow, ebb, inertia —
womb-weary the carcass waits
disintegration.

And Diana, bareface,
chills our intelligence
she, a classic case
pelvic and continent.

Waiting for the Ferry

Your voice sounds far away,
out of reach in a time beyond Greenwich —
the telephone demands yet more guilders
with a blinking insistence,
while informing me in five languages
that I can increase the volume of your voice
by pressing button B.
I do, and you sound closer to me
and as calm as this Dutch Sunday morning.

I will face the North Sea, headed in your direction,
with no navigational skill,
knowing there is no easy course
to reach you,
and that you may have quit the watch,
the empty seas.

'Take care', you say
as the last guilder drops
and I might risk it all
by trying to say the pent-up
regret, by trying to bring
the hope of you breathlessly
to speech in the dying seconds
of this conversation.
And you? You might perhaps
talk of pain and what is possible
but this strict Dutch machine
completely silences you.

Galway

Mellows surveys the junction with a kind of gray
and ineffectual simplicity,
petrified in an incisive rain.

Rumours of a beach
where shy feet
disturbed an afternoon sand.
Sunday at Salthill,
the acme of a country childhood.
The homing flushed and drowsed
with sea light and tang . . .
The sea is savage now
and a ship in the dark
eeks out into the night:
but the feet are tired
battling with origins.

Rain and the night is refaced,
wires laden down with rain
loop in the headlights.

An Atlantic of rainfall
cuts across the track, and is
for a moment held in the light-beams
before becoming a dark edge
to a red road.

The human cargo,
warm and word-laden,
takes on the inhospitable night
and moves out of the bay's inertia.

The Patriarch

My father was a butcher,
and before he killed his sheep
he beat them
about the head
with the sticking-knife,
held clenched in his fist.
I can still hear the wooden handle resound off the bone
and the sheep's eyes roll before me,
having smelt blood she tried to resist
being slaughtered —
of course it is a *she*: the meat is more tender.

With cattle he had a different tactic,
because a heifer could kill him
in that narrow cold slaughter-house,
so he took a very thick rope
(as I've seen holding tons of barge
to a mooring post along the canals of memory)
and laced it on her neck with frightened rage,
and drew the end through a huge link in the floor
and pulled that beast to her knees.
And then I should wrap that rope
about my childish waist
and keep all that vibrating flesh on its knees.
If I failed to keep my footing
he beat me across the face,
and through my silent tears
I saw him slow and distorted,
like a deliberate monster
load the humane killer —
a lovely name for a thick lump of deadly metal —
and place it on her forehead,
he squeezed the trigger and she fell
pulling the rope tighter about my waist,

but I could step towards her
and ease my pain, seeing the neat hole which never bled
above the dead open eyes.

The entrails of the dead beasts
warmed me in that place of terror
and their blood ran down my legs,
long before I woke to find
my own blood hot and sticky
between my legs.

Yes, my father was a butcher,
and kicked me down the stairs
before going to the slaughter-house
because he had no choice,
and I must know that I could not choose.
But he had all the strength,
and I kept my tiny rage
intact behind silent tears
until soon I overcame that too,
and there were no tears, just silence,
and blood dripping passed my eyes,
I saw him through it
and I saw red.

Was I four, or eight, or twelve,
when I loved him enough
to sit with him at the opera
and note his delicate skin
in the half-light, that handsome man,
that butcher for whom I felt so much:

even when they bound him
and took him away ungraciously
and called his dilemma by a clinical name,
I remained loyal, polite and dutiful
hiding my rage with life,
to visit and find his head wired
and his limbs kicking with electric shock.
This was treatment, I never saw it as revenge.

I felt only pity, deep unspeakable pity,
I glimpsed all the dead sheep and cattle
in him as he crawled along
the floor, on his hands and knees,
some rattling unvoiced awful sounds
in his throat, and his blue eyes rolled at me
as if life was being squeezed out of him:
I stood in the middle of that cell
while he crawled about me
and I felt the blood run down my legs.

I did not know
that if you take an eye or a tooth,
even if for an eye or a tooth,
that you must suffer the trauma
of losing an eye or a tooth —
if you kill, if you butcher,
you must experience the trauma of
killing and butchering.

And still no choice.
Just wonderful intellectualisms
to convince myself
that I could cope
with being butchered:
that I could understand
and explain it, and bear no resentments
as his eyes challenged me
to free him from
the confines of his cell,
to love him that much
and play Verdi on my expensive hi-fi
just for him, and partake delightfully
in all that pleasure.
No bitterness.

I simply showed all my bitterness
and all my anger to others,
especially to those for whom
I protested love.
I protected him.

Then last week I found him
partly paralysed,
his thundering right fist hung limp.
No need now to burn out
any more brain cells,
that fist will never rise again
to strike the defenceless.

He is now defenceless,
as he grips a tripod stick
with his left hand
and tries to stand,
and move cautiously
across the floor.

I do not fear that fist,
nor that hard black shoe.
He can still strike me
with his tongue,
and his words cut much deeper
than his hard black shoe —
I find my footing,
feel all the strength
that he has lost
invade my right arm
down to the fingertips.
Then I take the wide forceful angle
and strike into his face,
I hear the resoundng bone,
and his still handsome face
falls from me, his body sprawls
painfully against the floor —
and suddenly I am no longer
tethered by a thick rope
to a dead animal.

There is now more shock
in those blue eyes
than ever a raging beast
could cause breaking loose
in a slaughter-house.

I shall never look
into those eyes again on this earth,
and he knows before he dies
that I have chosen
finally not to be butchered.

Teach na nGealt

Seomra sceirdiúil
agus gloine na smolbháistí
idir lucht saonta agus an lá:
sinn de shíor ag siúl,
trom, trom, thar urlár snasta
nach scáilíonn ach draoibchrot an duine.
Tá an t-aer tiubh le boladh na bhfear.

Trí leadrán liath
an aolcheantair sínte romhainn amach
seálann an siabán an corrsceach.

Ar mhaoil na haoise ar a mairimid
tagann macalla traenacha
ag siollántacht chugainn mar chuisle na beatha
caillte sa cheobhrán
feiceann is ní fheicimid
na sraoillíní fada ceangailte
as imeacht a chéile
ó iargúltachtaí na díchuimhne,
trom, trom, thar urlár míntíre,
is na miondaoine sa smúid á dtarraingt
ar shlí an iarainn.

Bronnann na haistir aislingeacha
chugainn sna cillíní cuimhne
ach tá an cillín á chúngú cheana féin,
ní mhaireann ach mothú gan ainm
ar imeall an scáthnóiméid
an sceach agus an sceach drogaithe sa cheobharnach
ag fulaingt na foilmhe, cuisle ar comhbhéim
leis na preaba san aigne le fada
dulta in éag.

Mad House

A bleak room
A window glass of smudged rain
between the inmates and the day:
we are constantly walking,
heavy, heavy over the polished floor
which only reflects our muddy shapes.
The air is thick with the smell of men.

Through the grey insipidity
of the limestone region stretched out before us
the thick mist cloaks the odd bush.

We live on the edge of life
and trains echo towards us
vibrating like the pulse of life
lost in the mist.
We see and we do not see
the long drawn out things
tied into the movement of each other,
drawn from the outbacks of memory,
heavy, heavy across the inland floor
and ordinary people, in this
viscid mist are being pulled
along the iron road.

All the pleasant journeys we have made
well up in the cells of memory
but the cells are already narrowing
there remains only a nameless feeling
at the edge of the penumbra:
a thornbush, and another thornbush drugged in the mist
suffering the vacuity,
pulsing with equal stress
with the pulsing of the mind
long since
dead.

Fíricí

Is fíor go bhfuilimid inár suí
glúin le glúin in ollspás agus i ndíseart
an tseomra seo:
suíocháin, mion-bhoird, pat-leathar,
duine nó beirt ag trasnú an chairpéid
chun deoch a fháil.

Is fíor go bhfuil an ghrian
ag dul i dtalamh
agus an uain mar a d'iarrfá í a bheith
áit éigin lasmuigh.

Sea, tá chuile ní aimridithe,
na dathanna fiú, liosta agus neamhlonrach.
Titeann braon ceoil anuas orainn, *Bizet.*
Carmen bhocht á tachtadh i gciseadh na bhfrathacha,
L'amour est . . . caillltear a deifníd
i maolú an atmaisféir.

Lár na tíre —
amárach caithfimid filleadh ar fhírinne an tsaoil,
níl anseo againn ach aiteall idir dhá chúram.

Tá an t-am á mheilt againn
i gclapsholas seo na bhféidearthachtaí
gloine le gloine clingeann,
— beoir, branda — agus ólaimid sláinte.

Is fíor freisin go bhfuil solas éigin
i do shúil a eascraíonn as dlúithe an nóiméid
agus nach mbaineann le frithchaitheamh na gréine,
braithim teanga seo na súile
ina comhréir is ina castacht
i gcinnteacht na gcéadfaí.

Facts

It's true that we are sitting down
knee to knee in this huge deserted room:
there are seats, little tables, false leather,
an odd person crosses the carpet
to buy a drink.

It's true that the sun is setting
and the weather is just as you'd
wish it
outside somewhere.

Yes, everything is sterilised
even the colours, which are insipid and dull.
A drop of piped music falls down on us. *Bizet*.
Poor *Carmen* is being choked in the rafters,
L'amour est . . . her definition of love
is lost in the constricting atmosphere.

The midlands —
tomorrow we must return to reality
here we have only a break among cares and commitments.

We pass the time
in this twilight of possibility
we clink glasses — beer, brandy —
and drink each other's health.

It's true too that there's a certain light
in your eyes which comes from the compression of the moment
and has nothing to do with the sun's reflection,
I feel this eye-language
and its complex syntax
in the certainty of my senses.

Cad tá idir chamáin againn i ndáiríre?
Cúrsaí an tsaoil, cúrsaí ealaíone
nó an méid a dúirt an té a dúirt an méid a dúirt sé
faoi chúrsaí teangeolaíochta, bitheolaíochta, agus araile.
Nó an scéilín grinn nár chuala mé cheana, measaim,
agus an ruainne dúirse-dáirse a chaill mé, má chaill,
ná bí ag trácht, ní raibh fhios agam go raibh seisean
ina chomhluí léi siúd . . . cén bhrí ach . . .

Cé go bhfuil ár gcomhrá spíonta cheana féin
agus na gloiní diúgtha,
is an ghrian imithe as
níl an seomra seo ina dhíseart a thuilleadh:

féach, *personae* eile ag druidim inár dtreo
séis comhrá eile agus cuideachta,
is leanfaimid go léir ar aghaidh
ag blaisínteacht ar a chéile
ag iarraidh an béal marbh a choimeád ar an *libido*
ag ibhe dí nach bhfuil de dhíth orainn —
faitíos, féinmheas, fuíoll agus fuineadh.

Scaradh oíche is lae,
scaraimid óna cheile
beol ar bheol de réir an nóis.
Slán.
I gcónaí tiocfaidh muid slán de bharr cleachtaidh.

Téir, a thaisce,
tá mogall do shúile ag titim ar a chéile.

Codladh sámh.

What are we really discussing?
Life, art,
or what so-and-so said about so-and-so
about linguistics, biology, etc.
Or the little anecdote I haven't heard before, I think,
or the bit of gossip I missed, if I did,
don't be talking! Sure I didn't know
that he was having it off with her,
I wouldn't mind but . . .

Although our conversation has already become vapid,
and our glasses are empty,
and the sun is gone
this room is no longer deserted.

Look, other *personae* are coming towards us,
more chat and company,
and we'll all continue to taste each other
pretending the *libido* is no problem,
sipping drink we don't really need —
fear, self-respect, consequences, playing down.

Night separates itself, day breaks,
we pull away from each other
pecking each other on the lips as usual.
Goodbye.
We always come through, we are so well-practised.

Go darling,
your eyes are already closing.

Sleep well.

Aithne

An chaoi a chasann tú ar an tairseach,
súil thar ghualainn agat
féachaint an bhfuil focal ar urlár?
Sa chasadh sin aithním thú
agus an nóiméad:
faic ar urlár, foilmhe,
na cairde go léir a theipeann orainn,
na freagraí agus na ceisteanna nach ndáiltear orainn,
agus na cuirí ar fad nár cuireadh riamh.

Maidin ar bith, is mí-éifeachtach gach stampa
agus is scannalach gach nóta
i bhfeadaíl chaoil fhear a' phoist.
Clac, coiscéim, clac eile a shonann
i gcoinne ná ndoirse dúnta.
Tafann teasaí béal dorais, clac,
coiscéim, agus coiscéim eile ag dul in éag —
lig leis an mhaidin í fhéin a dóirteadh isteach ort,
tagann sí i gcónaí gan chlúdach, gan lorg fraincéala.

Is fearr agus is fusa b'fhéidir
teacht ar an urlár mín um thráthnóna,
urlár fadfhulangach a chasann macallaí
ár gcoiscéimeanna féin ar ais chugainn,
macallaí a dhiúltaíonn an taom áthais, an t-éirí croí sin
roimh bhille fiú, nó roimh scéilín beag breallach
ón Roinn.

Cruthaíonn ár n-ainm is ár seoltaí
go bhfuilimid ann, nó in ann,
nó in ainm is a bheith ann, agus
go bhfuil duine eile áit éigin lasmuigh
nach mbaineann leis an dream seo
atá ag coiscéimíocht thar urlár cistine linn —

Recognition

The way you turn on the threshold,
glancing over your shoulder
looking for a letter on the floor.
In that turn I recognise you
and the moment:
nothing on the floor, bareness,
all the friends who have failed us,
the questions never put, the answers never given,
and all the invitations which were never sent.

Any morning at all, a stamp is ineffective,
and there is something scandalous in every note
the postman whistles.
Clack, footstep, another clack
reverberates off closed doors.
Heated barking next door, clack,
his footsteps die in the distance
let the morning pour itself in on you,
it always comes without an envelope
and without a trace of the franking machine.

It is better, and perhaps easier
to face the bare floor at evening,
that long-suffering floor which casts back to us
the sounds of our own footsteps,
echoes which deny a wave of joy,
a rise of the heart, even for a bill
or an insipid little note
from a government department.

Our name and our address prove that we exist, or are
capable, or at least we are capable in name.
It proves too that there is someone else
out there who has no connection
with this gang of ghosts walking across
the kitchen floor with us.

An dream sin a thionlacann gach céim,
gach casadh, agus gach ceann-fúinn.
Is ionann an dream sin agus gach deis
nár thapaigh muid chun laincisí
an chuibhrinn seo a réabadh,
is ionann iad agus an réabadh fhéin,
agus a chroí dhil, is ionann an dream sin,
ar aon choiscéim linn
agus leimhe an éalaithe.

Fan, mar a fhanann muid i gcónaí,
ar fhaitíos go dtitfeadh an dea-scéal
ar urlár tréigthe.

Tuiscint

Preabarnach trí dhuilliúr, traein,
tá an fómhar san fhoghar —
ach ní shonann traenacha a dteannas ionainn
a thuilleadh, na himeachtaí, an eagla
go litríonn dúinn an dul ó thinteán seo
an t-imeacht gan filleadh.

I mothú an aeir tá an míshuaimhneas —
an tuirse, an t-uaigneas, an tocht,
an deoir is an deoraíocht
ag stáisiún oileánda éicínt,
tá an greannfhocal ag an nGiolla — lá bog —
anamúlacht gan anam, nach cuma,
a liacht díobh a tháinig faoi raon a shúl
paisinéirí gona rún chun an iarnróid
is an béalrá as an duibheagán docht
ag brioscarnach
súla dtagann go laomtha sa léithe á síneadh féin
an phéist.

Those ghosts who accompany every step we take,
every turn, every slight dejection.
They are our lost opportunities
to break this isolation, this entrapment;
they are the break-out itself,
and above all they are the let-down of the escape.

But wait, my dear, as we always wait
just in case the good news
might fall on a deserted floor.

Intimation

Train-pulse through leaves,
the air, the tone, autumnal —
but the trains no longer tense us
wording the goings off, the fear
that this hearth-leaving spells for us
the one of no return.

Unease in the air-sensation —
tired, lonely, breastladen,
tear of the exile
at some isolate station,
the easy Porter jokes — soft day —
kind and insensitive, and why not,
so many has he seen
shy passengers coming to the rails
trite talking out of the unspeakable
gap before in the gray lit elongating
comes the worm.

Níl Guth Agam Ort

Is féidir liom labhairt leat ón leaba.
Stánann na deich bhfigiúr orm
ón ngléas idirbhealaigh, brúim,
comhcheangal na matamaitice —
ligeann an gléas geoin bheag as
i gcuisle agus i dteanga nach dtuigim.
Sos meicniúil —
dóirteann do ghuth isteach orm
ón taobh eile, ón dorchadas atá ag líonadh
an spáis eadrainn:
comhaistriúchán
ach níl mise ná tusa ann.

Cé go bhfuil guth eile dod fhreagairt,
agus is liomsa é, táim ar fán
na mílte míle uait, agus uaim fhéin.
Briseann mo ghuth i mbristeacha beaga cainte
ó shiolla go siolla san fhoilmhe,
ach tá an guth scartha uaim, bíodh agat é,
mar ní litríonn mo ghuth mé.

Ach seachain, a chroí, seachain,
ná fiafraigh, led' thoil,
cén chaoi bhfuilim
ar eagla go bhfaighfeá freagra ionraic.

Freagra a réabadh fál an dorchadais,
agus atá de shíor ar imeall na bpreaba
leictreonach a líonann do theach
ón gcéad tuin go dtí an scoilt critheaglach.

Mairimid faoi scáth agus faoi choimirce
na teicneolaíochta,
gan sa mbaint seo eadrainn
ach siollabacht an scéil,
tá fhios agam nach bhfuil a thuilleadh uait.

I Have No Voice Against You

From my bed I can speak to you.
The ten digits stare at me
from the telephone, pressing,
I make a mathematical connection,
the apparatus drones — murmurs something
a pulse and a language
I do not understand.
A mechanical pause —
your voice pours in on me
from the other side, from the darkness
which fills the space between us:
A mutual translation of us,
without us.

Although a voice answers you,
and it belongs to me, I am adrift,
millions of miles from you, and from myself.
My voice breaks into fragments
syllables in the void,
but my voice is disembodied, take it,
because my voice does not spell me.

But careful, my dear, careful,
please do not ask
how I am
you might get an honest answer.

An answer which would shatter the
wall of darkness, that is always
on the edge of the electronic
pulses which fill your house
from the first tone to the terrified break
of the circuit.

We are at the mercy
of the technology,
in this connection between us
there is only the sound of syllabics,
and I know that you have no wish
for more.

Colfairtí

I gcónaí thar mheán na hoíche
nochtann an tairiscint
sna bearnaí beaga intinne
leagan an féileacán oíche a sciathán
go héadrom ar an gclaí gloine
arís agus arís eile, níos tréine
mothaím
plabanna beaga a chinn
i gcoinne na fuinneoige
chomh neamhéifeachtúil liom fhéin
nuair a chuireann an léas drithleach
an tsúil faoi chluain:
cuirtear chuile rud eile ar ceal,
an chiall, an eagna fiú
a chuardaíonn muid i gcónaí
beag beann.

Cinnte, déanfar luaithe díom
go beo beathach,
b'fhearr liom loscadh i do theocht rua
agus críoch a chur
ná bás a fháil i bhfuacht ghloine.

Ní raibh mé istigh aréir
ach tháinig mé air, ar maidin,
is mé ag filleadh slán
ó chuardach agus scaipeadh na hoíche
ceann-bhrúite os comhair m'fhuinneoige
is an deannach daite
ag sileadh óna sciatháin.

Rejections

Always after midnight
the offer is made
in the interstices of the mind.
a moth lays its wing
lightly on the window-pane.
Again and again, stronger now,
I feel it strike its head
against the window
as ineffectual as myself
when the light gleams
and seduces the eye:
all else is abolished
sense, even wisdom
for which we search so much;
to hell with it.

Certainly, I shall burn to ash
but I should rather burn
in your red-hot intensity
to the end
than die against the cold glass.

I was out last night
but I came on it this morning,
as I returned intact
from the search and dissipation of the night
a battered head at my window
— the luminous dust —
fallen from the wings.

Muigh Inis. Mí Eanáir

Seasaimid triúr
ar na crompáin ghainimh
gealacáin mhara fúinn ar fhís,
tá an tsúil ina sclábhaí don tíreolas
agus do chumhacht na cluaise.

Tá an tost tite.
Tachtann an tafann an focal.
Sinne, trí chorp stalctha i ndrad na gaoithe
faoi na bristíní solais san aer spréite
nach lá é, nach oíche,
lastar smid fiacaile, leid súile
ach druideann an fabhra
tá an béal iata.

Téann toirnéis an nóiméid i bhfeidhm orainn
seantuin
an cnámhfhocal.

Thángamar na mílte, má ba mhílte iad
nó scáileanna suain
pictiúrí fánacha
mar a bhfuil an chnámh curtha as amharc
i bpuiteach an Achréidhe,
agus an oidhe seo nach oíche romhainn
in aon tafann amháin taoide
anois, agus i bhfad i gcéin —

An Teach Dóite, Ros Muc, Cárna,
chomh haduain lena n-ainmneacha.
Scairdíní solais ag spiacladh na smúide
is an bealach á chasadh
i gcoimhthíos na carraige scrabhaite.

Mweenish. January

We stand, the three of us,
on the sand dunes
bright bits of sea visible beneath us,
the eye succumbs to the lie of the land
and is enslaved by it
just as it is enslaved by the power of the ear.

Silence has set in
The sea barks and chokes all words.
We are become three bodies chilled by the wind
under particles of light spewed into the air
it is not really day, not night,
an eye and a tooth gleam for an instant,
but an eyelid closes to
the mouth is shut tight.

The commotion of this moment confounds us,
the old tune
skeltonic.

We have driven for miles, not measuring,
perhaps they were shadows of a dream,
stray images
there is bone buried out of sight
in the mud of the Great Plains,
this night and its lamentation
is a roar of filling tide
here and echoing in a far distance.

Maam Cross, Ros Muc, Carna,
as strange as their very names —
little clusters of light against the dark
along the road which twists itself
among an inhospitable and scarred rock.

Seo againn í:
an t-ionú iomlatach as tromluí lárthíre
an fharraige
deireadh thiar.

Deannóid salainn ar mo bheola,
na beola seicimínithe
Sonann an chasúireacht ó na clocha aníos
iad réidh, sleamhain-chraicneach,
beidh an charraig ídithe fiú —
fágfar na púróga daite ar an trá
don ghrian scólta.

Bhíomar anseo cheana agus ní raibh —
tá an chis inmheánach bánaithe
i strus an bhob á bhualadh,
an mhuir chríonna, níonn sí an bith nocht
as an sliogán agus níonn
na siollaí as an gcloigeann.

Tá na cianta geabacha i ngéibheann
sa rithim rómhór,
líonn an Ghuthaíocht an garbhimeall
gan i ndán don siolla bríomhar teacht i dtír.

Dorcha-dhán ar an duirling,
smugairle róin urlachta i measc an turscair
i gcrónú an ama.

After all that
we come out of a midland heaviness
to a huge inundation
and find the sea
finally.

A taste of salt,
the lips are already dry.
The rocks underneath
are even and smooth
hammered into shape,
yet even the rock itself will be dissolved
and reduced to coloured pebbles
left for a scalding sun.

We might have been here before
in some former life
but the meshes of memory are plundered
in this sea stress.
The old sea which rips the living thing
naked out of its shell
and it rips the word from the skull.

Centuries of speech are reduced
to nonsense in this huge rhythm,
distorted voices cry and are broken into tiny bits,
not one single syllable of meaning
survives to landfall.

There is a sibilance in the shingle,
and somewhere perhaps there is a jellyfish
cast and tossed in the seaweed
to die in the advancement of time.

Muid balbh ar an láthair seo
nó go nochtann duine againn ár náire
le loime a labhartha: 'Tá sé fuar.'
Tá.

Casaimid
cúl cinn leis an agallach
agus feicimid den chéad uair
glaschloch an oileáin —
na crosa ina gcloigne ceilteacha
ag gliúcaíocht thar an bhalla amach.
Ab bú búna!

Braitheann an chos
mísc na míne gainmhí
á meilt.

Slán. Aige. Linn.
Cuirimid beirt an bóthar lomtha
dínn athuair, cé bocht ár spré,
ach téann an fharraige is an focal suain
in árach a chéile
i gcnámh linn
an t-am go léir.

We are dumbfounded here
until we are exposed in sparse speech:
'it is cold' —
it is.

We turn our backs on this sea-chatter
and find for the first time
the whinstone of the island
peering out over the graveyard wall.
Ab bú búna/o me miserum.

Underfoot
the sand is rough
and erosive.

Goodbye. To him. With us.
Two of us leave along the bleak road
though our insight is slight,
the sea and the sleeping word
conflict within us,
somewhere deep in the bone
for the duration of all time.

Samhradh

Samhradh, roimh ghuth ar ghéag,
sula sracann an domhan chun solais
sula n-éalaíonn an bhrionglóid ó screamh na súl —
ina sciathán an scáth
sa chaoch.

Samhradh, meán lae,
tá cailín san abhainn deirtear,
trí mhíle thuas, aréir,
ag cuardach a coirp táthar,
thar an droichead a chuaigh,
tríocha bliain síltear,
ina haiteachán riamh —
smut, francach ag snámh
crapann craiceann abhann,
trost faoin mbád
téann bloc adhmaid
tharainn
le sruth.

Samhradh, tráth luí gréine,
lag-leoithne gan roic ar abhainn.
Beach chun deiridh
ag guagaíl as blad lusa,
filleadh agus flaitheas na n-éan
ar eite chun barr crainn,
an lá ag cruinniú a choda leis,
foilmhe san atmaisféar
agus goic ar an nóiméad
go bhfuil mórtarlacáin an tsaoil ag tarlú
in ascaill gach dúna i bhfad san imigéin
agus an uair láithreach seo ligthe i ndearmad.

Summer

Summer, before a voice breaks on the branch
before the world reaches the light
before the last dream leaves the eye —
the shadow of a bat
flits across the blind hollow of dawn.

Summer, midday,
there is a girl in the river, they say,
three miles up, last night,
they are searching for her body,
she jumped off the bridge,
thirty years old they think,
always a bit odd —
snout, a rat swims
and the skin of the river contracts,
something thuds against the boat.
A lump of timber
floats by us with the stream.

Summer, sunset,
soft breeze now, not a wrinkle on the river.
A late bee
backs out of a flower,
birds return delighted with themselves
to the tree-tops,
the day gathers itself for going,
it is an empty feeling
and the moment sits
as if the great events of life
are happening somewhere else far away
and this present here has been forgotten.

éalaíonn an ghrian . . .
cling ar chling
aithníonn muid blosc binn an tséipéil,
fearann an clog fáilte,
buille ar bhuille
aiceann ar aiceann
méadaithe ar an abhainn
ach seang a fhriotal dá bhíthin.

Anocht
caoi ar ghrinneall, glas ar dhoras
cuirfear
agus luífidh sí sa taobhroinn.

The sun slips away . . .
cling, cling,
we recognise the chapel bell
as it welcomes,
its measured tone
is made resonant and full by the river
still, it sounds slim and disturbing.

Tonight
the river bed will settle back
the chapel-door will be locked
and her body will lie in the side-aisle.

Beir Beannacht

D'éalaigh tú thar chiumhais na maidine,
ní nach ionadh
bhí an t-éalú ionchollaithe i do theacht.
Fanaim
ag comhaireamh na mbáisteachaí thar an fhuinneog,
sileann an t-am.

Ritheann sé liom go bhfuil duine éigin
ag an doras, téim:
asclán bláthanna, aghaidh choitianta, fear
in éadaí dubha —
sea, is mise, domsa, duitse —
spréann na feileastraim in a gclaimhte,
lasracha gorma ina bhaclainn aige.
Nach rídheas an mhaise duit
an lá a chur trí thine.

Iris — teachtaire na nDéithe
cuireadh go *Díodó* í san anallód
leis an aon fhuascailt amháin
d'éinne atá ag lúbarnaíl ar an mbreocharn
agus *Aeinéas* imithe leis chun a dhán
a líonadh.

Anois
níl fágtha ach leid an mhiotais:
na feileastraim sínte ar an mbord
agus faoin mbord sínte
faic.

Tá do chailleadh gan chorp.
Ní féidir an fhoilmhe a chur faoin bhfód.

Fare Well

You crept away over the edge of morning,
no great wonder really,
the going was embodied in your coming.
I remain
counting the rains which fall across the window,
time spills.

It occurs to me that
there is somebody at the door, I go:
a bouquet of flowers, a common face,
a man in dark clothes —
yes, that's me, for me? For you.
Irises, spread, spears,
blue flames across his arms.
How lovely of you
to set my day ablaze.

Iris — messenger of the gods,
she was sent to *Dido* long ago
with death, the only relief
for a body writhing on a pyre
and *Aeneas* gone off with himself
to fulfil his fate and keep word.

Now
there is only left a hint of myth:
irises stretched on a bare table
and stretched under the table
nothing.

Your loss is without a corpse.
There is no burying an emptiness.

Ar M'Éirí dom ar Maidin . . .

Caolann an oíche chun na maidine,
sileann an solas, sileachán faoi choim,
diaidh ar ndiaidh trí fhallaing na fuinneoige:
ní féidir é a sheachaint maidin ar bith.
Téann na silíní solais i dtreise
go réidh, go héifeachtúil, gach cúinne, gach log súile,
briseann an lá ar chiumhais coinsiasa.

Doicheall agus déistin fiú
tabhairt faoi in athuair,
sa neamhní neantógach seo
is scriosach gach smaoineamh
agus is seasc gach léargas anama.

Cos thar chois amach,
agus buailim cic i ndraid an lae.

Getting Up

Night narrows itself to morning,
and light spills surreptitiously
little by little through the woven window:
there is no way to avoid it or the morning.
Light shafts strengthen slowly,
effectively, every recess and corner, every eye-socket,
day breaks on the edge of consciousness.

Reluctance, loathing even
to take it all on yet again
in this nauseating nothingness
when every thought is treacherous
and every insight is impotent, every breath barren.

Stepping out,
I kick the day into the teeth.

II

Siúlaim trí sheomra na rang

Siúlaim trí sheomra na rang
gan ceist ar bith,
is mithid dom éisteacht,
fanacht, mar is fadó a bhí
siad caillte i dtaibhreamh na gceacht
agus i gcogarnaíl na haislinge
a d'oscail an domhan uile dóibh
trí chrot na fuinneoige,
trí mheán na bhfocal,
trí shlíocadh na coise slime
thar chláracha an urláir.

Tagann monabhar na nglóracha
chugam a fhanann ar uachtar boird
agus a chloisim i mbarr na méaracha
á gcuimilt ar an adhmad
a bhfuil tásc na mblianta air —
binnghuth na gcianta.

Aoibhinn bheith anseo
i measc na scoláirí,
gan cumha dá laghad ná dubh-chuimhne,
mar líonann tú an seomra,
gealann tú an clár dubh
agus coinníonn an fhuinneog
d'aghaidh ina creatlach.

Amuigh faoin aer
i gclós na scoile —
chomh halluaiceach,
teann, tnúthánach
is a bhíomar riamh mar scoláirí—

teipeann ar theanga na súl.

I walk through the old classroom

I walk through the old classroom
without a question.
It is better for me to listen
and to wait . . . it is so long ago
since pupils lost themselves here in their lessons,
and in the whisper of the dream
which opened up the world to them
through the window frame.
and through language,
and the slender bare feet
slipping across the floor-boards.

The echo of their voices
comes to me and rests on the desks,
I hear it with my fingertips
as I rub the old timber
which carries the mark of years.
This echo is the sweet voice of the centuries.

It is so pleasant
being here with the ghostly scholars,
I feel no sadness, no dark memories
because you fill the room
and brighten the blackboard —
the window holds your face
in its form.

Outside
in the schoolyard
we remember just how lively,
strong and eager we were as students —

and suddenly eye-contact is not enough.

Anois tá an lá cúrtha i gcrích

Anois tá an lá cúrtha i gcrích
agus codlatach,
is fadó a bhris sé ar na codlatáin
mar a bhris na miontonntracha
ar a gcosa i gcomhaontas na hoíche aréir,
ar imeall na farraige móire.

Leánn na laethanta go léir ar fad
a bhaineann leatsa
in aon sleamhnán amháin ama
gan idirdhealú, ná cuid de,
ó bharr go barr na céime cosligthe —

Moillíonn muid taobh thiar de na dumhacha
a fhanann idir sinn is an fharraige
atá ag búireach ar an taobh eile
agus ag druidim go díbhirceach chun na trá
a thuile agus a threabhadh
le racht suáilce.

Druideann muid féin go réidh
thar na dumhacha amach,
agus faoi sholas na gealaí
síneann an fharraige a méaracha chugainn
cóiríonn sí slí shíobhtha shínteach dúinn.

Titeann ár scáileanna uainn
ar shobal airgeadúil na mara

agus tá an diamhair dothomhaiste.

The day is put to its end

The day is put to its end
and exhausted,
a long time ago it broke on those who slept
just as the waves broke
at their feet in the alliance of last night,
at the edge of the ocean.

All days that have to do with you
melt into one continuum of time
no breaks, no distinctions,
free and unfettered
we move forward.

Behind the sand-dunes we have delayed a little,
away from the sea
which bellows on the other side
as it bounds into the beach
to fill it and to ruffle it
in a fit of frenzy.

We move out easily
over the dunes
and under the moonlight,
the sea stretches fingers to us
and the sea smooths our path.

Our shadows fall away from us
on the silver foam

and everything else is immeasurably hidden.

Briseann an ghrian trí rosamh na maidine

Briseann an ghrian trí rosamh na maidine,
maidin mhánla Mhárta —
tá borradh faoi chuile ní,
ach bailíonn an lá a chuid leis:
tusa.

Táim gan splanc i do dhiaidh,
táim gan splanc i do chuideachta.

Ritheann mé ó sheomra go seomra
chomh mear le míol Márta
b'fhéidir go bhfuil fiú cíor nó ciarsúir,
rásúr nó ríbe gruaige fágtha
i gcúinne nó i gcófra,
rud beag, neamhbheo
a dheimhníonn dom
nach raibh tú liom faoi dhraíocht
nó faoi dheismireacht:
ach go raibh tú liom.

Tá an teach fós tonnchreathach.

The sun breaks through the haze of the morning

The sun breaks through the haze of the morning
—a gentle March morning —
everything is expanding,
but the day takes its portion with it:
you.

I am crazy without you.
I am crazy with you.

I dash from room to room
like a mad hatter,
perhaps you have left a comb, a razor
or a rib of hair somewhere, anywhere
in a corner, in a cupboard,
anything small and inanimate
that will prove to me
that you were not with me magically
or that it was a fantasy,
but rather that you were with me.

The house still lurches from side to side.

Sonann do ghuth

Sonann do ghuth
gealgháireach
am lóin,
am briste aráin.
Glacann an lá sos
súla gcasann sé
chuig a chéad mhír eile.
Déanann an lá rud orainn
nuair a ghlacann sé
go fial
leis an lá atá le teacht.

' Sé fáth ár n-aoibhnis ná
gurb ionann chuile lá
agus inniu
agus gurb ionann chuile chomrá
agus an comhrá
atá á chothú againn
anois
láithreach.

Your voice sounds

Your voice sounds
radiant
at lunchtime.
A time of breaking bread.
Even the day pauses
before turning
to the next part: afternoon, evening . . .
The day does us a favour
when it accepts graciously
the next day that is coming.

Our reason for delight is
that every day is today,
and that every conversation
between us
is the conversation
we are having this minute.

Bhris an mhaidin

Bhris an mhaidin
ar aistíl álainn an tsneachta,
domhan íon
ar an domhan tite,
agus an saol uile séimhithe.

Is ionann an aimsir láithreach
agus siorradh sneachta a thagann
ón áit aduain sin
a luíonn i bhfad uainn,
chuig an nóiméad seo
in a bhfuil chuile ní féideartha.

Morning broke

Morning broke
on the peculiar prettiness of snow,
a pure world
fallen on the world,
and all of life subdued.

Present time and tense
is a snow-sift come
from a strange place,
from far away
to this very instant
in which all is possible.

Siúlamid ar comhchéim

Siúlamid ar comhchéim
thar chosán caol na coille,
rúndiamhaireacht ár rithime
ag cur is ag cumasc le chéile,
casann na crainn an macalla
ar ais chugainn
i ndíchéidmheacht na hiarnóna.

Téann traein thar bráid fúinn —
toll torannach,
chomh scíobtha sin, athluann sé
féin, arís, is arís, is arís eile
fad is atá sé ag imeacht uainn.

Titeann an t-uisce
braon ar bhraon,
glacann an linn leis
ag tnúth leis an tuirlingt:

gan braon uisce
gan linn lách
bheadh caoincheol
an tsílidh
dochloiste
anois
agus san am atá le teacht.

Sileann do ghuth
dochreidte
agus téann sé
i mbeo agus i mbeatha ionam.

We walk in step

We walk in step
on a narrow woodland path,
our movement composes
its own secret rhythm,
trees cast the echo
back to us
in an afternoon
beyond belief.

A train passes underneath —
a thunderous sound,
so rapid it says itself
again, and again and again
in its going away from us.

Water falls,
drop after drop,
the pool accepts each drop
with longing:

without a drop of water
without an accepting pool
the trickle of sound
and its soothing rhythm
would remain unfelt
now
and in time to come.

Your voice flows and soothes
unbelievingly
and goes
to the very core of me.

Moillíonn tú i gCill Mhantáin

Moillíonn tú i gCill Mhantáin,
briosc gaoithe ar d'aghaidh,
ní choraíonn ní ar bith eile
seachas do ghuth i gciúnas sléibhte
agus i n-uaigneas gleanna.

Téannaim féin sa treo eile
chun na farraige síos
i bhfad uait —

Méadaíonn an gleann do ghuth
agus tagann sé chugam ar mhinicíocht rúnda
ar chuisle na hiarnóna
ar phreaba na rothaí
a nglacann an bóthar chucu
agus a ligeann an bóthar céanna uathu
in aon chasadh amháin.

Braithim thú i d'aonarán seal idir dhaoine,
agus feicim do shúil ag léamh na spéire
mar a léann an tsúil gheal chéanna
rún m'anama.

You linger awhile in Wicklow

You linger awhile in Wicklow,
facing into a crisp wind,
nothing moves or has life
but your voice in mountain silence
and in the aloneness of the glens.

I go in the other direction
down to a western sea
away from you —

but the glen amplifies your voice
and it comes to me on a special frequency
on the pulse of the afternoon
on the rhythm of the wheel
which takes the road
and lets go of it again
in a single revolution.

I feel you alone awhile in the world,
and your eye reads the sky
just as your eye read and scanned
that lone part of me.

Mé sa ghluaisteán leat

Mé sa ghluaisteán leat,
cogar i leataobh: searc,
easpa anála.
Aon fhocal? Deamhan focail
a chuirfeadh an nóiméad seo
trí thine duit.
Ach tá greim láimhe eadrainn,
teanga eile i mbrú tráchta . . .

In the car with you

In the car with you,
a faint aside: love,
a held breath.
A word?
 No word
to set this moment on fire.
But hands find each other,
another wording
in a traffic jam . . .

Spréann an spéir romhainn amach

Spréann an spéir romhainn amach,
agus tá na scamaill á gcuimilt
i bhfialtas agus i bhfónamh na gaoithe—
foltscaoilte
agus muidne ar aon dul leo
faoileanda
gafa i luas géaraithe
i dtreo scál na gréine
sula n-imíonn sí uainn
le suaimhneas Domhnaigh.

Chomh lúcháireach is atá tú
taobh liom,
is no focail go léir ligthe ar lár againn,
caidreamh is cuideachta á gcothú
nach mbaineann le haltadh na cainte
toisc go bhfuil an chaint féin
agus gach aon chuing
scaoilte —
luíonn gríos na gréine ort
luím féin i do luaimhneacht
lonrach
lántoilteanach.

The sky spills out ahead of us

The sky spills out ahead of us,
clouds touch
in the strength and plenty of the wind —
dishevelled clouds.
We move with them
seagull-like
held speeding
towards a sunburst
before the sun itself slips away from us
with a Sunday stillness.

How splendid you are
beside me,
all words left and let go,
there is an intimacy connecting us
which has nothing to do with articulated speech —
that which binds speech,
and all other bonds and ties
are loosened —
the sun glows upon your face
and I give easily to the impetus,
clear
and full of consciousness.

Éalaíonn do ghuth uaim

Éalaíonn do ghuth uaim
siar thar na mílte eadrainn,
agus feicim thú ag casadh leathanaigh
cois boird.
Go séimh, glacann tú le réalaíocht an nóiméid:
ní mór . . .

Suím anseo, freisin cois boird,
i mbeocht agus i gcroíúlacht d'íomhá,
ag caomhnú na bhfocal a chuir tú chugam
sna focail a chasaim chugat ar ais.

An t-idirnascadh sin —
gurb ionann gach focal uait,
gach leid, gach samhail
agus athchruthú an fhocail bhunúsaigh
ráite agat
i raidhsiúlacht na hiarnóna
agus muid leataobhach don lá
ar an tsráid chomónta
i gcoitiantacht na ndaoine a chuaigh
thar bráid gona gcásanna féin
á dtionlacain, gona léargais féin
ar comhchéim leo . . .

Tráth luí siar,
tráth dhúnadh lae is leathanaigh
táim fós faoi iontas is iomlánú.

76

Your voice slips away from me

Your voice slips away from me
over the miles which stretch between us,
and I image you
turning pages at a desk.
Quietly you accept the given.
We must . . .

I sit here, also at a desk,
enlivened and made animate by the image of you,
cherishing the words you have sent
in the words I return to you.

This combining —
every word from you,
every hint, every metaphor,
is a remaking of the fundamental word
uttered by you
in the expanse of an afternoon
while we stood as an aside to the day
and the common street
and the generality of people passing by
with their own cares accompanying them,
and their own insights in step with them . . .

When lying back,
when closing the day and the printed leaves
I am still full and full of wonderment.

Braith mé thú inné

Bhraith mé thú inné
i lár na coille
ag baint suaimhnis
as an ollchiúnas,
agus bhraith mé thú
i gcoiscéim an Earraigh
thar chlaí . . .

San idir-thráth insínte

San idir-thráth insínte
glacann an t-anam
chuile ní chuige féin
ina dhuibheagán.

Téann gné is gné eile
den rún-taithí
i bhfeidhm air,
agus luífidh sé, mar anam,
i gcinnteacht an nóiméid
atá le teacht
nuair a chuirfeadh sé
gach aon mhionghné
den phantasmagoria
i gcóir is i gcrích.

I sensed you yesterday

I sensed you yesterday
deep in the forest
taking pleasure
in the immense silence,
and I sensed you
in Spring slipping
along the hedgerow . . .

In an extended interim

In an extended interim
the mind takes
everything to itself
into its vast immensity.

Every aspect
of the intimate experience
touches the mind
and it will remain reserved
holding its secret to itself
until there comes a time
without conjecture
then it shall arrange and finally define
every aspect
of the phantasmagoria.

Is bronntanas na maidine thú

Is bronntanas na maidine thú —
an chaoi ina gcruthaíonn sí thú,
guth, mion-ghluaiseacht, gluaiseacht,
athrú aoibhinn anála,
tá sí mar mhaidin chomh leochaileacn leat,
líne, imlíne, fíorimlíne —
baineann sí thú aniar as an oíche,
chomh séimh sin is a dhéanann sí é,
chomh ciúin, socair.

Ansin cruthaíonn sí briongláin na gcrann
os comhair na fuinneoige
agus griogann sí an madra chun tafainn.
Cruthaíonn agus cothaíonn muid a chéile
i gcomhairle agus i gcion na maidine.

Glacann an tráthnóna thú
ar ais, arís,
nuair is gá duit
casadh ar leac an dorais
agus tabhairt faoin mbóthar
atá le dul eadrainn.
An bóthar céanna
a shíneann chugam agus uaim
in aon síneadh amháin.

tá na maidineacha chomh míorúilteach sin,
tá an lá ar fad agus an oíche
fite iontu
gan chuimse.

You are a gift of morning

You are a gift of morning —
the way it creates you,
voice, a little movement, movement,
a delightful change of breathing.
Morning is so delicate with you
a line, an outline a real outline —
she draws you back out of the night,
she does it so gently, so quietly,
steady and unruffled.

Then the morning creates the branches
of the trees at your window,
and she starts your dog barking.
We create and nurture each other
in the affectionate influence of morning.

But the evening takes you back again,
you must turn at the door
and drive back the road which stretches
between us.
That same road which leads to me and away
from me in the same movement.

But the mornings are miraculous,
the entire day and the night
are woven into them
limitlessly.

Sonann do ghuth fós

Sonann do ghuth fós
i m'chluas,
tuirse na hóige
tar éis ard an tsamraidh —

briseann an fharraige
ar chósta an Oirthir fiú
agus ritheann sí le gean talún
chun an t-inbhear a líonadh —

tuile, taoile . . .
slaparnach na mionuiscí
nuair a chasann an mhaidin ort
cois trá

tonn faoisimh
á mbriseadh féin
ar an duirling

Ritheann na blianta go léir
chuig an nóiméad sin —
líonán lán leathan
nach bhfuil faoi laincis
an leathchoda,
ní dhearna tú leath riamh
agus ní dháilfeadh leath ort
maidin Earraigh
nuair a chuirfear fáilte romhat,
a chroí.

Your voice still sounds

Your voice still sounds
in my ear,
youth tiredness
after the heights of summer —

the sea breaks
even on the east coast,
and slips in, seduced by the land
and fills the estuary —

flooding, tiding . . .
small waters swash
as morning turns towards you
by the beach

a wave of ease
breaks itself
on the pebbled shore

all the years, and the years
run to this moment —
swelling full and wide
unhampered
by half-measuring,
you never measured your giving,
and giving will not be measured for you
this spring morning
in the welcome which awaits
you, beloved.

Tá fuadar faoi na druideanna

Tá fuadar faoi na druideanna
os comhair m'fhuinneoige,
ag tógáil as an nua
agus ag teacht i seilbh a sean-eastáit
atá fós slán iomlán tar éis an tséasúir.

Nach méanar dóibh filleadh
le fuinneamh fionnuartha.
Cothaíonn a ngníomhaireacht
athbheos ionam maidin Chéadaoin
agus tusa ag saothrú leat
i líofacht do lae.

Is soilbhir agus is soilseach thú
i gcroí na cathrach,
faoi bhun do shaothair.
Braithim thú soineanta, soiléir, gairmiúil.

tá na druideanna fós ag canadh
ar ard a mbinnghuth,
agus tá muid go léir gafa
sa chomhdhéanamh saothrach.

There is enterprise

There is enterprise
among the starlings outside my window —
they are building anew
and repossessing their old estates
which are still intact after the season.

Isn't it delightful for them to return
with refreshed energy.
Their action activates a new life in me
this Wednesday morning,
while you exert yourself
in the expanse of your day.

You are bright and cheerful
in the heart of the city
earning your keep
I feel you calm, clear and professional.

The starlings are still chattering
at the top of their sweet voices,
and we are all involved
in a busy structuring.

Casaim cnap an raidió

Casaim cnap an raidió
agus táthar ag casadh do cheoil.

Líonann tú is líonann an ceol
cluas an tseomra seo.

Ait mar atáim gar don chlúid
is méanar duit faoin dtuath,
ait mar atá tusa
cuachta sa chathair.

Aoibheann mar a thagann
do ghuth chugam:
cian-cheol do chruthaíochta.

Labhraíonn tú liom ón leaba,
suaimhneach, sínte
tar eis an lae iomláin.

Táim fós á chumadh agat,
beireann tú greim ar an oíche
agus a leochailleacht.

Anois titeann néal beag codlata orm,
tá an tsúil á dúnadh
i séimhe an tsuaimhnis . . .
casfar sinn ar a chéile
nuair a chasann an oíche
ar chosán ard na gréine
ar maidin.

I turn the radio on

I turn the radio on
and they are playing your music.

You and your music
fill this listening room.

Odd that I am now
so close to that place which nourishes you,
odd that you are
wrapped and bound within the city.

Your voice comes
and gladdens me:
the far-sound of your creativity.

You speak to me from your bed,
stretched and restful
after a completely full day.

You are still creating me
as you take hold of the night
and its delicacy.

But sleep slips in
and an eye closes
in this tenuous time of ease . . .
but we will meet
as the night meets
the morning
along the sun's highway.

Fanaim cois farraige

Fanaim cois farraige,
cois cuain lán lagthonntrach
a ghlacann an spéir chuige.

Téann scamall nó dhó
thar bráid gan deifir ar bith
idir mé agus an beann a luíonn uaim.

Tá foileán agus faoileán eile foluaineach
ós mo chionn
ar mhionghaoithe a thagann díreach aniar chugam
as an gcúlra sin a bheathaigh muid
agus atá fós ag beathú na gaoithe.

Seachas an ghaoth féin
is follasach go bhfuil an lá ina stad
cé nach bhfuil an tarraingt siar feicthe
agam go fóill,
cé go bhfuilim aineolach air mar chúlú,
agus aineolach ortsa,
díreach sul má líonann tú an lá
agus an radharcra.

Ach i dtuiscint an chúlaithe
agus i gcomhlíonadh na huaire
is féidir linn dul in airde
go barr binne
agus sracfhéachaint a thabhairt ar an gcuan
sínte romhainn amach ina dhearadh is ina chrot coimpléascach.
Réithímid an lá le chéile, taobh le taobh,
ag teacht ar dhearcadh úr-nua
a d'iomlánódh an t-am romhainn agus an t-amharc fúinn.

I remain by the sea

I remain by the sea,
by the wide and weak-waved harbour
which takes the sky unto itself.

A cloud or two
passes by with ease and no speed
between me and the far-off promontory.

A gull glides by, then another
overhead
on a minor wind which comes
from the west:
that place which nourished us,
that place which still nourishes the wind.

Except for the wind
the day has clearly come to a standstill —
although I am still ignorant
of the withdrawal,
unaware of the pull back,
unaware and ignorant even of you,
just before you fill the day
and the view.

But in the understanding of withholding
and in the fullness of time
we can climb to the top of the hill
and look back down on the harbour
stretched beneath us with a complex shape.
We solve the day together, side by side,
reaching a new aspect
to complete and make whole
a time ahead of us
and all that lies beneath.

Cois tine

Cois tine,
i dtaca na meánoíche,
an domhan uile
ligthe i ndearmad:
gal móna
galú buartha
nach aoibhinn dúinn
bheith soiprithe.

By the fire

By the fire,
a midnight hour,
the whole world
left and overlooked by us:
turf smoke
and no trauma
there is such pleasure
in being nestled.

Tá na duillí beaga

Tá na duillí beaga
ar bís agus ar hob pléascadh
i gcantaireacht an chlaí;
is deora beaga iad
ar bharr brionglán
ar fhís go tobann romham —

dearmad déanta agam
go raibh an spionnadh nua
á phreabadh in umhlaíocht chlaí
i gcuas an tráthnóna
is mé ag comhaireamh mo choiscéimíochta
i macalla an uaignis
i bhfad uait . . . síneann an t-achar . . .

Ach anois ba bhréa liom dul amach
láithreach, cé go bhfuil an oíche tite
ar an gclaí cheana féin,
agus greim a bhreith ar an Earrach,
is a bhorradh, é a bhailiú i mo bhaclann
agus a bhronnadh ort
sul má éiríonn tú
ón talamh báite
i scread na n-inneall
ar eite uaim
chun go mbeadh
teocht an Earraigh agat
i do thuirlingt, a chroí,
ar thalamh an oighir.

The tiniest of leaves

The tiniest of leaves
are about to spring and explode
through hedge song;
they are like tears
on the tips of twigs
suddenly come into view —

I could overlook
such vigour
pulsing in a hedge
in the recess of evening
while I counted my footsteps
echoing in isolation
far from you . . . time stretches itself . . .

But now I could go out
though night has already fallen
on the hedge and on the world
and catch the Spring
and the fresh upsurge
and gather it into my arms
to give to you
before you leave
this rain-soaked land
winging away from me
in a scream of engine
so that
you might have the ardour
of Spring, my dear,
in coming in
to an iced land.

A thaisce

A thaisce,
tá do cheist léite agam,
táim féin dall
ar an iomlán;
caithfidh tú
deis agus deis eile
a chothú dúinn agus don dán
agus tiocfaidh tú ar an bhfís
atá i bhfolach ann.

My dear

My dear,
I have pondered your question,
I too am blind
and cannot see conclusions;
you must
create and allow a time
for us and for the underlying pattern
and then you too will come
to clarity.